D0776615

ENGLISH LIT

POEMS BY
Bernard Clay

OLD COVE PRESS • SWALLOW PRESS

Old Cove Press
Lexington, Kentucky
oldcove.com

Swallow Press / Ohio University Press
Athens, Ohio
ohioswallow.com

Copyright © 2021 by Bernard Clay. All rights reserved.

Paperback ISBN: 978-1-7352242-7-5
Electronic ISBN: 978-1-7352242-6-8

First Edition

To obtain permission to quote, reprint, or otherwise reproduce
or distribute material from Old Cove/Swallow publications,
please contact our rights and permissions department at
(740) 593-1154 or (740) 593-4536 (fax).

Versions of the following poems have appeared in:
Appalachian Heritage, 'Allergen'
Black Bone, 'The Good Couch' and 'Learning to Cuss'
Feel It With Your Eyes, 'The (Un)seen'
Leo Weekly, 'I Still Ride the TARC'
Limestone, 'Urban Oasis' and 'Anotha Kick Theme'

Printed in the United States of America
Old Cove Press/Swallow Press books are printed
on acid-free paper ∞ ™

Library of Congress Cataloging-in-Publication Data
Names: Clay, Bernard, author.
Title: English lit : poems / by Bernard Clay.
Description: Lexington, Kentucky : Old Cove Press ; Athens, Ohio :
Swallow Press, [2021]
Identifiers: LCCN 2021015739 (print) | LCCN 2021015740 (ebook) |
ISBN 9781735224275 (paperback) | ISBN 9781735224268 (pdf)
Subjects: LCGFT: Poetry.
Classification: LCC PS3603.L3863 E54 2021 (print) | LCC PS3603.L3863
(ebook) | DDC 811/.6—dc23
LC record available at https://lccn.loc.gov/2021015739
LC ebook record available at https://lccn.loc.gov/2021015740

To the unseen

Contents

ENGLISH LIT

FIELD TRIP

a first-grade excursion
to the zoo becomes a safari
through the neighborhood
that surrounds the school
that most of my classmates
are bussed to every morning

we barrel through dense poverty
and lush decay
some kids bury their gaze
into seat backs like ostriches

some kids leer out the panes
eyes popping like lemurs
some kids look back at me
like i'm a gazelle chased by a cheetah
surrounded by lions

misreading their attention
i act as an exotic guide
answering questions
about the flora and fauna
even pointing out my home
to a collective gasp
and pity glance
then the chaperone mom
steps in, *i lived there, too,*
before this place went to hell
all the kids' mouths

3

are agape like hippos
then the mom's face
turns baboon-butt red
and she apologizes
for swearing

the rest of the way
through industrial parks
we fog the windows
singing 'old macdonald'
like a flock of egrets
and one crow
until we get to where
the real animals are

CORPORAL TRAINING

it starts at home
hand to butt   simple enough
then escalates as you grow
     green switches open up legs
     then belt welts back
     then palm swells cheek
     balled fist quakes skull
and what always followed:
i did it 'cause i love ya
and you begin to build calluses

first grade your nervous teacher
     recommends you for psychoanalysis

second and third grade you're strategically paired
     with two surrogate *mammies*
     to control you

fifth grade white teacher
     got to paddle you
     like a true hoosier deserves
     two paddle whacks
     and a denzel 'glory' tear
     down your cheek

then at that age when
     you could be charged as an adult
     nightsticks press into your sternum
     while you watch a mother's head

get driven into blacktop
as her son's throat is slowly closed
with a boot
because he was loitering

all this while
you've been building calluses
        but those calluses aren't baton-proof
        they are reminders
        you will see later on
                when people
                who look like you
                get routinely
                beaten and snuffed out
                in your daily media feed
        to not expect
        any *i love you's*
        from this world

HOMES AND VACATION (also my assimilation)

i used to come to campus an outsider
partitioned off from the traditions
excluded from the upper levels
of the ivory tower

but soon the lushly landscaped
sphere of isolation
was an open-ended vacation
from the metro granite planet
where i was raised

and as credits accumulated
cinder-block dorm rooms
graduated to off-campus apartments
which seemed more like home
than mom's red-brick tenement

where just to sleep on the family couch
i needed to place reservations
which i often had
walking my old streets

ENCHANTED ROTUNDA

in the capitol rotunda
of this once 'switzerland' of the states
the men of historical stature stand
all sculpted from solid bronze
crowned around lincoln's
brown effigy
his backbone mettled
cape thrown, ready to strut
all six feet, four inches of lanky body
onto the great lawn
to free the slaves again and again

but behind lincoln   a traitor rose
conjured by jim crow wizardry
chiseled from white tennessee marble
the president of a figment
jeff davis, self-proclaimed mississippian
his chalky hands vice gripped
rigid body cocooned within his cloak
his eggshell gaze looking
down on lincoln's head

only in that rotunda did
jeff davis tower over lincoln
there, davis was the only labeled 'hero'
on his exaggerated pedestal
which redacted the rivers he ran red
with the blood of the poor

whose children's children's children
made sanctioned pilgrimages there
bussed from the hollers
and the cul-de-sacs
to pose at davis's milky white feet
because this   (they were told)
is their heritage
this   is what makes them great-(er)

THE (UN)SEEN

I am the only black
in this gallery
on an MFA field trip
to write about art

My focus is locked
on the sole image
that reflects me,
a black and white photograph
titled 'Hog and Gun'

The photographer's gaze
passes over the shoulders
of three men facing
into the shadowed kill box,
their gun aimed
at two swollen pigs
bleached stark white by the camera
as the black rifle barrel
recoils off the gelatin
and everything else colored
is flattened
into an invisible grayscale,
like the three granite-skinned men
in this picture who look like my kin

Here, like those men
I am both obvious
and overlooked
framed so far in the foreground
that I am background

YOUNG AUTHOR

he didn't know the rules
but he did know
that words were a promise
between us and the universe
to fashion our world
out of the stories we tell

from birth, he loved bending
and stretching the taffy of existence
taking loose clucks
and utterances
and mastering language

crowned the liar king
by relatives, he told tales
rolled so tightly in lies
and baited half-facts
they assumed every word
was fiction

at school his first-grade teacher
took rare interest
in channeling
his 'untapped' energies
into the state-mandated
young author project

and his backbone quickly aligned
with the cardboard spine
of his handmade graphic novella

it detailed the gruesome demise
of his three pet hamsters
(which, in reality, were only two
and a lot of goldfish, all of which
died *suspiciously*)

self-illustrated
images included
an orange rodent-like crayon blot
with dead double-x eyes
inside a large scarlet circle,
a tan and white oval
with a pink whiskered snout
leaping into an open
heating vent,
and a portly brown blob
with profuse buck teeth
labeled 'pookie'
flippantly forgotten
by the boy's mother
trying to claw its way
out of a basement aquarium

and while the reception
by the class
was mixed
from fear-tinged laughter
to outright disturbance
his mom was tickled
by the last page

she put his first
and only edition
on the mantle
with treasured
photo albums
and prom pictures,
laughed and said,
'boy, you know
i didn't kill that rat pookie!'

GETTING SHARP

every sunday evening
daddy seized the living room
for his ritual
the whole time his eyes
would be tethered to
60 minutes or *knight rider*
or even *murder, she wrote*

first, he'd lop off the iron pokers
plunging from his nostrils
then scrape an old razor down
his bristled face sounding like
metal across concrete
then he'd wax that fat
salt-and-pepper mustache black
twisted into villain-curled tips
'cause, no woman
wants some old man, he'd say
taking his gaze
off the tube
only to lose it
in the porthole mirror
reflecting himself

he'd buff and varnish
for a whole tv show until
my snaggletooth smile
reflected back
in the many pairs

of oxfords and loafers
lining the living room,
buzzed off the kiwi paste
he'd say, *shoes are the second thing*
the white man's gonna judge you by,
ain't nothing you can do 'bout the first
he'd point to my forearm
so you better get the shoes right

finally, he would unfold
the arrowhead board, firing up
the hot flat anvil to stab across
a week's worth of button-up shirts
until they were as thin
and crisp as papyrus
and if momma wasn't around
he'd lean over and whisper
you'll never get a good lookin' woman
with bunchy-ass slacks, boy
then he'd grind his wool
suit pants into a razor's edge

TV LAND

i'm born into a neighborhood
a chrysalis of brown faces
and early on i avoid
the warmth of the blue flame
beamed into our living room
consumed nightly by family
i prefer flipping through
a good picture book or hearing
a toothy story from mom
and i wonder why
my family watches
those flat pearly-faced
blabbering people
who i doubt
are even real
because i never see them
around here
or maybe i don't recognize them,
like ancient westerners never
saw the color blue until nubia
introduced indigo to them
then blue began to permeate
from the sea to the ether

first morning of first grade
is my indigo day
i plunge into a lunchroom
crawling with tiny tv people
only not quite, their skin

isn't luminescent lily
like the cameras portray
it ranges from pale seafoam
to barbecue pork rind
with dark veins below the surface
their heads are lumpy
their features are asymmetrical
and the room reeks of baloney

i sit down among them
and like it is rehearsed
a 'flesh-tone' band-aid
of a boy blurts, 'my father
says your skin's like that
because y'all don't wash'
cue: laugh track of entire table
were tv people dumb in real life?
confused i ask, 'are you all du— ?'

but before i can finish
the cafeteria monitor
swoops in with her
crisco-white tight
roller-set afro
and she snarls
with her buttery
tank-tread teeth
'as soon as i saw you
i knew you were trouble'
cue: laugh track of entire cafeteria
she apprehends me

removed to a tiny table
our backs to the room
i'm with all the other ones
who look like 'trouble' too
all boys
all rode my bus
and behind us
the tv people are everywhere
like the oceans   like the sky

GRANDMA'S GREENS

on the forgotten side
of a babylon
is where grandma's garden hung
shadowed by silo mountains
in earshot of smoky iron rivers
we left the asphalt
to spend the growing season
with her
our young knees
bent into turned earth
we built foliage cities
of collard, mustard, and turnip
by tossing embryos
in ancient gridded rows
as grandma chanted incantations
and bushy jade heads
sprung from the dirt
to swallow sun

the grandbabies' jobs were
to harness aluminum clouds
to precipitate on the leaf palaces
to mine weeds with bent tridents
to defend the veiny structures
from critters
but once the plants got waist high
grandma would tell us
to decapitate them all
to the altar of kinfolk

and on the rim of dusk
in a screened-porch temple
over a carpet of newspaper
we pick their sturdy flesh clean
from spindly stalks
squash any bugs
then have her anoint our offerings
with her thorough inspection
before she marches
every emerald bushel
into her cauldron
of rolling aromatics,
roots and spices,
the greens scream a bit
hitting the boiling water
their leathery texture
softens as they drown

sending out unseen signals
to relatives all the way in newburg
down to alabama, houston
even my home blocks away
the hairs on our necks stand on end
when another pot brews
and sooner or later we find ourselves
around a too-small table
in a too-small house
and everyone's just fine
we can't resist the polarity
of those steaming plates
of grandma's hocus pocus

that she passes like an heirloom
across several generations

even after her matriarchal reign
grandbabies and their babies
will practice the high art
of potioning greens
and conjuring family

BARBER COLLEGE

let me cut them sticker bushes, boy
said great aunt eva
short, sturdy, and smocked
in her own barber shop
as she placed me in a booster seat

and, boy, give me some shugah, too
her whiskered lips pecked
at my toddler cheeks and then
she began excavating
my head   I cried

she'd point at
the many photographs
proliferating across the walls
of a broad man who sort of
looked like my daddy

see, boy, he's your cousin
see, boy, he's the champ
                of the whole world
I'd look at daddy
and he'd shrug it off
then I would whine to leave

one day daddy up and said
your aunt eva never gives
the cut I want

so he brought home
a wahl's clipper set
to d.i.y. my head
at the dim kitchen table
no pictures on the wall
of anyone here
and with no training
no instruction
daddy dove in

I heard
a lumpish snort
before I felt
the hot vibrating razor
glance off my skull
before I saw
a black cloud of my hair
sink into my lap
then *oops, sorry!*

next day momma sanctioned
daddy and me on an emergency
sabbath morning haircut
to stave off church embarrassment
we went to the 'big a' strip mall
entered a wood-paneled shrine
to u of l cardinal basketball
and also to that man
aunt eva called champ

every square inch of wall
had either a red bird
or him, satin-shorted and shirtless
with shimmering sepia skin
while on tv played
a vhs tape of this poetic warrior
boxing through reporters
and pundits and peers
his whole career on infinite loop

when I got seated
the barber asked me loud enough
for the whole shop to hear
you know that you and your daddy
are blood with the greatest?
he pointed at the tv
I shrugged it off like I was taught to
did your daddy not tell you about him?

I shrugged again, daddy looked away
the barber shook his head and said
we gonna fix that
then this blade wielding homer
proceeded to spin an epic tale

Cassius descended from Titans out of the Hades part
of Louisville, like you and me and all of us

said to have Hephaestus hammer fist, to be as swift
as Hermes especially in the lip, and prettier than Helen

kidnapped at an early age and trained in Troy
by a pantheon of mere men rich off their daddy's inheritance

their new Achilles whose heel was having an IQ so low,
by their design, he could avoid Vietnam

and if he stayed in line, he'd be their next
Mr. Bojangles-Jack Johnson

but Cassius wasn't their Atlas for long
though he was a brown Delphi

predicting then delivering Liston to the mat
and putting his benefactors into a cash coma

and as they slept, post-fight, Clay's Trojan-horse chest
opened and Muhammad Ali coolly strolled out

a soon-to-be black demigod tongue-launched
fiery barbs at the oppressors' press

torching contracts, introducing black folks to self-love
especially after that cabal went after that heel of his…

but that's another odyssey
for your next cut, young one

there's almost a standing ovation
and I yearn to stay in the chair
and hear more from this sage
but daddy is already paying and he interjects,
all he did was trade one master for another
that shows how weak-minded he was
changing the family name and all

everyone gets quiet
the barber curls his lips in disbelief
and says, *you just jealous*
'cause you still got that clay money
which ain't shit compared to that ali money
and the shop erupts in laughter and jeers
at my daddy who sort of smiles
gives an almost defeated nod
then tips the man as we slink out the door

LEARNING TO CUSS

a boy named man was my first best friend
momma said they made him in a project
he would ghoulishly grin
even as he choked out his pet doberman
        with a fat gauge chain
even as he rained hot piss on my face
        from the treetops giggling thunder
even as he crunched into my little sister's
    ʹ   forehead like a red delicious
but see   back then best friends
were like daddies
you're stuck with forever   i thought
so i mirrored man, to keep the peace outside
just like at home

and that day was no different
i replicated man's every action
every sound
we skipped crushed colt-45 cans like stones
across the street into the curbs where older kids
        stood, ignoring our childish insults
then man grinned and hurled a rock
        and two words   made of
        four javelin-tipped syllables
they pricked the attention of the teens and adults
        until they saw it was *just li'l man being bad*

but he had their attention and i wanted it, too
so, like a toucan, i mimicked man

now the first word i knew from tv
        it meant momma
but that second word was fresh, primordial
        i had to bite into it
        to form that 'f'
        and when i did
everything stopped   everyone's face stopped
        in disbelief

it was almost cinematic
how the whole block mobbed up
to drag my ragdoll body
to my big bad daddy
as kids gleefully chanted
        'aww, you in trouble,
        your daddy's gonna whup you'

and as i was stripped and lashed with a belt
        by my daddy on the front porch
for a neighborhood audience to see
through a blurry veil of tears i saw man
        grinning at his composition as daddy wailed
and that's when it sunk in   that's when i swore
to never be like either one of them mothafuckas
        ever again

WHEN I FIRST MET MYSELF

i'm in a back yard
no words to process
just   me   smelling sun
pouring out the sky
tasting every flavor
of green in the grass
that orange-breasted robin
in front of me
bouncing
and i'm bounding
behind it barefoot
stroking its velvet soft feathers
in my mother's garden
at our old house
on beech street
this is the beginning
of my reel
my raw footage

i'm still absorbing
when i get
to the herb side
and chive is in bloom
purple lollipops air-light
basil pleated leaves
dancing
serpentine thyme
grounded and
twisting into loops

the garden rows
are shelves of life —
strawberries
green beans
yellow squash
tomato spiders
aphids and swallowtails
fingertips nibble
at velvet butterfly wings
stalks and vines sing and wrap
and my eyes spin like tape,
recording it all, no filter
no context

then momma comes out
in a rosy robe
with pink sponge rollers
parachuting from her head
wagging her finger
and chucking words
like furniture at me
but words
are meaningless
only her arrow-pointed face
darting at me matters
she grabs me up and yells
'you know you know better than that!!!'

only i never really will know
better than this   anymore

THE GOOD COUCH

in the living room
sat the couch
one of them splurge items
an oatmeal tweed burlap thing
purchased spontaneously at value city

and for the good-couch reason
my parents covered it
with a sheet of plastic
a foggy heavy synthetic skin
that rustled with every motion

when summers smothered up
scorching hot days
back when home a.c.
was a myth to me
something not felt
but alluded to on tv

on those simmering evenings
primetime bubbled across
blue flickering screens
couch filled to capacity with family
and box fans propped in windows
making our house
a convection oven

we would broil on that couch
as its transparent epidermis
bonded with our bare
arms and legs
so that, of course
i would have to wait
until the next commercial break
because the sound of me ripping
clean from the velcro couch
would've drowned out the tv a bit
and everyone would have thrown a fit
'cause cosby
might have said something witty
in his air-conditioned brownstone

BEDTIME STORIES

mom abandoned fairy tales
and fables of old ladies and shoes
and racist-ass dr. seuss, too
early on   she says i got bored

she expanded into the bookcase
saved for impressing visitors
and big sisters' school projects

started with the searing
electric-blue children's bible
twenty-two books covered
with bearded khaki men
on a beige jackass or camel
'full-color' illustrations
from adam and eve
to jesus resurrected
but   by kindergarten
those stories bored me, too
though i accepted their simple
good or evil worldview

i then jumped into
the twenty-seven volumes
of world book encyclopedia
many an early adolescent buzz
was had off the intoxicating
aroma of binding glue and words

as i worked my way
from aardvark to zygote
enamored with east and west
cultural conquest
of savage places beneath

but something about those
world books did not ring true
i never saw me in them
i felt like a boil   hated
invisible   societal canker
mom warned i was too young
for the last book set
all the way to the left
hard bound in brown like me
the covers branded in gold
with *afro-american encyclopedia*
and the *ebony* magazine emblem

the first time   i opened it
to a black and white picture
of a lawn full
of paper-colored people
smiled and posed
and picnicking
a huge tree was center frame
and from it hung man-sized
licorice-twisted pods
in half-scorched clothes
smoke and souls piping

off the contorted masses
and i slammed
        the book shut

but   time after time every night
i kept going back
to those ebony books
that made me mad, made me scared
made my story truer

THUMPER

walking home
from my third-grade
christmas pageant
where i bombed
two solos
daddy scooped up
this flatulent
bag of muscle
half pit bull
half boxer
half tongue
we named him
from the movie *bambi*
'cause when happy
his tail whacked
at anything
like a cartoonish big
rabbit foot
clapped ground
he would break out
run around
to all the homes
brave and free
to feed
licking new faces
his giddiness infectious
and i envied him
even at that age

because
that was once me
before
but like my old self
eventually
he, too
was stolen
by the world

CORNER STORE

they build interchangeable temples
to our endorphins on every corner here

at first I was ordered to go
but soon i was volunteering
for those daily *filter kool* runs for dad
up the street to that key lime
cinder block shop
draped with a constant macaroni
necklace of cars at the drive-thru
fronted by a concrete garden of statue men
kissing paper-bag medusas

the alley behind it is a casino
with money pots often left
when cops raid

wrapped in cartoons and lore
i flock with the fructose fiends
jittery off jolly rancher jolts
primed for stronger buzzes

see, our gateway locks
are busted open
well before we get a whiff
of the 'really' addictive stuff

28TH AND CATALPA

in the eighties
on walks to the bus stop
mom would fill in the exposed
empty burned out spaces
of entire city blocks
augmenting reality
to a pre-riot state

        so where mom sees
        a soda fountain shop
        tasting the bubbly bite
        of root beer, waited on
        at the front counter
        (instead of getting it to go
        at the back door)
        as she watches the bustle
        of brown pedestrians
        in business attire passing by
        like this is baby harlem

i see nothing
but a headless structure
with graffiti-boarded eyes
on a twenty-year death fall
into a puddle of bricks

and over there
at that department-store-sized
gunshot wound
at the corner of 28th and catalpa

    her eyes take her shopping
    at the black-run department store
    she peruses phantom aisles
    trying on polyester garments
    at the only department store
    she's allowed to (at the time)

    and across the street
    at the cinemaplex
    she sits in the front row
    (not the balcony)
    flinching her way
    through seven watchings
    of hitchcock's 'the birds'

i just stare through
the dead theater's scorched
rib bones jutting up
from its shelled carcass
the gray louisville skyline
barely visible through the murk

mom would sometimes say
        'they tricked us into thinking
        separate was bad
        we get that reminder
        every time we walk
        through this place
        so we can pay bus fare
        to reach *their* equality'

as we wait
in this haunted crematorium
which in the morning fog
still smoldered
like it did the day after
king was assassinated

IROQUOIS PARK

on some fall saturdays
after hours of being trapped
in a prison of droning
designed to shame me
mom broke norms and sabbath
we'd leave the stained-glass early
invite my bff to sleep over
pick up a box of wings and wedges
from indi's, avoiding dad
for the afternoon
and heading out to that mound
south of the city

after eating, while mom lay on
the picnic table and read long
neglected *jet* magazines,
laron, vette, and i approached
that hulking hill before us
that we likened to a porcupine-
leviathan, like the one that ate jonah

and we ran full speed at it
got swallowed behind its jawless row
of tulip-poplar teeth
and let the dense honeysuckle
seize us deeper into the belly
of those woods
we kept charging through and up
to its limestone-blowhole-lookout point

to view the skewed city spiderwebbed out
to every horizon
then we'd chute all the way down
the persian rug of gold
and orange leaves on our backs
the city and everything else falling away
eventually getting down to mom
my eyes thunder stormed
my shame gone

then we'd go home
and if   sports were off
and if   daddy's teams had won
then right before snl's cold-open
he would give laron and me
the *whose-daddy-makes-*
the-best-popcorn? quiz
we'd answer *you do, of course!*
that newfangled microwave corn
of laron's suburbia
couldn't stand up
to daddy's hot-out-the-pot
masterpieces
each buttered and salted
handful a crunchy blessing

EARLY PHILOSOPHIES ON BEING
A SEVENTH-DAY ADVENTIST

very early on it lured me in with candied light beams
from windows of cherry, lemon, and sour apple
with snacks in the toddler lounge while grown folk
recited seventh-day adventist tenets
it got me with the swaying in unison   hymnals opened
organs growling   piano plucking   as words, which at
that age are a cage to me, sprout wings in my throat
and take flight, flocking with the other voices becoming
one in the rafters of the church

by the time i was old enough for sabbath school
when the teacher said jesus:
     walked on water
     raised the dead
     and would herald the second coming
          of heaven on earth

already my response was:
     i tried walking on water and almost drowned
     not sure why i care about dying, i'm only six
     and i could have heaven on earth
     right here and now
          if i could stay home sabbath
          to eat bacon egg biscuits
          and watch saturday morning cartoons

talk about salvation

HAIBUN FOR MAGAZINE STREET CHURCH

o, magazine, your services are a journey through meaningless circular sermons of *turn the other cheek*. i protest with my feet kicks to the backs of pews, finger flicks to clip-on ties, and from the balcony i crash church-bulletin paper airplanes into the backs of hats and fascinators. weekly sabbath dinner socials in the basement are canned veggie-franks and lawry's seasoned green beans to salinate our souls, as red kool-aid magma bathes our brains and catapults us out onto the parking lot, a pissing contest for show-offs that i win by all the kids telling me to get away because their parents say i need to be medicated.

my rock nails a sweat-bee nest
sister's mouth gets stung
i get my ass whipped

DINNER AND A MOVIE

born in a son sandwich
stacked between sister slices
raised and protected by a tired mother
who always tried
cable TV matinees
babysat us a lot
like empire of the ants
starring Joan Collins
about giant radioactive ants
devouring an island of resorters

my little sister age four
me age six
after watching
we ran outside
me to the front yard
to unleash a holocaust
with a hand-held
rainbow prism reactor
I laser pinpointed
solar napalm across
all the ant hills in my yard
irradiating every
tiny leathery thorax
into ash
my face warping
into a drooled smirk

then from the backyard
my little sister regally emerged
her outstretched arm
a long velvet sleeve
of creeping black specks
her face crackled with discovery
as she asked,
have you ever ate ant heads before?

then she grabbed a mouthful
from her forearm
and proceeded to eat
a whole battalion

then like a cereal commercial
she cheesed and said,
they're pretty darn good!

KINKY BIRTHRIGHT

A hundred thousand mothers
before Mitochondrial Eve
her hominid ancestors
had their heads battered
by the equatorial sun so much
that their skin built a wall
out of pigment and perspiration
then fur thinned to hair
and cobra coiled around
large craniums tight
each wiry strand clenching
to beads of profuse sweat
until the sun evaporated it
which air-conditioned their primate brains
just enough for them to evolve into us

Growing up
all my sisters saw
our locks of inheritance
from the first mother
as a lifelong burden
enduring years of third-degree
chemical burns and scalp scabs
to straighten 'that stuff'
into a lifeless pelt
more suited to survive this
colder climate and society

Then they would style
using a plutonium rod
called a curling iron
which they would
casually lay blistering
on my favorite couch cushion

Too bad I squandered
those two million years
of intellect—
maybe it was too much TV,
maybe my close shaved
summer cut robbed me
of my natural refrigerator-coils —
somehow I forget that it's the 1980's
that I'm wearing short shorts
and I forget about looking
before I take my coveted seat

And you know
it's true what they say
about that third time
after hearing your ass crackling
like bacon on a skillet   twice
after having the entire family
convene like primetime
around your butt   twice
as your mom bandages your gooey
scalded flesh   twice

That third and last time
is for sure the charm
and you now look
for the rest of your life
before just plopping down
anywhere

Thirty years later
my posterior scars faded
now   none of my sisters
voluntarily singe their scalps
on a regular basis
just to conform
now   they all
wear their hair like Eve

FIREWORKS

my mom left the old man, dragging us behind to
even lower-scale housing deep within the west
end where these four kids lived around the corner,
one girl and three boys, dead bolted into a paper-
mache house next to a liquor store. my bedroom
window overlooked their trash cluttered backyard,
two floored-mattresses were their beds, hot fries,
jolly ranchers, and check soda their diet, and
their parents lived life shoved into the narrow
chambers of soot-tainted glass pipes.

i was so jealous of those kids, they didn't have
to brush their heads or teeth, lived with both
their parents who never raised their voices to
tell the kids what they could not do. the parents
lived mostly on the porch, smoking cigarettes,
staring off, looking like they were about to cry, or
in jittery conversations with anyone that would
listen. but they somehow could obtain new
jordan's on release date and kept the trendiest
outfits at the top of that drastic unisex hand-me-
down pyramid.

those four kids threw jokes at my old converse
and my snug church-school uniform but we still
played together out of necessity. i filled their
bellies with kool-aid and cookies, they showed me
conditional friendship playing flag football with

the outcast. even my little sister got to play with
the girl's name-brand barbies.

then that fourth of july, on the six-hour drive back
home to my mom's for a holiday hiatus during the
old man's summer of custody, as legally agreed,
we drove through tennessee where the gunpowder
fireworks were for sale, and dad pit-stopped to
take us divorce-christmas shopping through the
catacombs of dynamite. we filled the whole basket
and i imagined the bounty was going to be enough
to make them kids jealous for once.

we got home and the kids greeted us with a brag
about ll cool j concert tickets tomorrow night
and their new british knights and just broke
out laughing at my new kim brand high-tops.
but when dusk hit, me and the old man ignited
white-hot cascades onto the pavement, propelling
roman candles, bottle rockets, and sparklers
into the sweaty night, exploding from red paper
scribed in gold chinese characters, as four sets
of eyes fastened on us, yearning to light. but i
didn't let 'em, not a single one, just a surge of gray
smoke rolling down the street that left their faces
contorted.

the dazzling light show lingered on my glowing
eyelids that night as i slept. the next morning, i
awoke to a smoke enshrouded window, the kids'

house next door was barely visible, distorted
and partial, and i wondered if that deadbolt
was still locked. immune to sirens, i missed the
dawn emergency call to that house, i missed the
four ash-covered bodies being carried out from
the smoldering shell, two found melded to the
mattress, suffocated mid slumber, the other two
with their fossilized hands grasping for that sealed
deadbolt.

later that day mom sent me back to atlanta with
the evening edition, the front page showed both
parents looking dazed in front of that charred
house, the paper reported they came home to
check on the kids after a late-night party and the
house was ablaze. they tried to open the door
but it was too hot, they lost everything but the
tickets for the ll cool j concert. but us from around
there knew those parents forgot how fire worked
and schemed for concert tickets instead of basic
utilities because candles are cheap, then left them
kids locked in on a rock run in the corner of night.

back at the old man's, i tried to sleep but my
eyelids still glowed like it was fourth of july. if only
i had let them kids light the fireworks, had kept
them outside a little longer, maybe glowed eyelids
would not have been the last thing they saw. that
night and for several nights after, i could not keep
my eyes closed, and i hated that i had that luxury.

THE LAST BLOCK PARTY

it's coming like puffs of mesquite
stampeding down the street
from the grilled teeth
of rusted half barrels
coming like finger pokes
through cling-wrapped bowls
of potato salad
or macaroni and cheese
picking the block's best dish

it's coming like type 2 diabetes
and orange push-pop mustaches
peddled by the sticker-tattooed
ice-cream trucks
barricading both ends of the street
whistling dixie in synth

it's coming like fanned bicycle cards
smiling blind ten wins
across burn-blotched tables
winking beer bottle spider eyes
as the spades champ is crowned

it's coming like a needle switch
to a spun black-wax universe
like subaquatic off-the-wall basslines
oozed out of porch-bound speakers
intertwined with michael jackson's

falsetto disco death croak
as little girls leap between
twirling double helixes
of rainbow-scaled snakes
whose plastic bodies
thwack sidewalk on beat to
can't stop 'til you get enough

but you hardly ever know
when you're at the last of something
there's no notification
except for the blurring
of the slave catcher sirens getting louder
and people heaped on people
heaped like fleshy lego walls
around him   splayed
in the street
the lopsided crimson polka dots
of his white t-shirt
getting bigger and redder
and beneath him a perfectly round
dark polished pool
opens wider and wider
swallowing the body first
and then everything else   whole

HOUSE LISTING: 1522 HEMLOCK
(with seller notes)

Early century Arts and Craft bungalow:
    deep concrete porch
    coal chute *(lockout work-around)*
    only two owners
    HVAC *(minus the AC)*
    back porch *(half-fallen, colonized*
                    by a mischief of rats)

One bedroom:
    big enough master for a king-size
    (will block) closets
    with doors *(from fully opening)*

One bath:
    shower-less spa tub
    big, mirrored medicine cabinet
    easily handled four *(ungrateful)*
    women *(hair-doing, makeup)*
    for ten years

Converted attic:
    two rooms one closet large enough
    to sleep three girls and a boy
    asbestos free most of the lead paint
    gone *(chewed up by the boy)*
    and great big *(box-fan sized)* windows
    for summer

Unfinished basement:
      completely finished *(unstocked)* bar
      mostly dry with laundry
      (and a tendency to flood
      with sewage during downpours)
      big enough *(to be an indoor pool)*
      for the kids to play

Huge backyard:
      completely shaded *(bald)*
      by a fence line of trees
      perfect for off-street parking
      (as car theft deterrent)

Gem of a house only reason I'm selling
(my no-good wife said she didn't need me no more)
I'm moving to Atlanta *(where she wanted to go*
but couldn't afford) to become a preacher
so get this place at a steal

SCRAPPED BOOK

when they bought me
i wasn't a predator
i was a book-bound eternal lockbox
of family moments frozen, disorganized,
but always there on the side of the couch

they broke me out to embarrass
to jog a story loose or just prove a point
and as the years passed
i got fat with those 5x7 morsels
until i became volumes of pivotal milestones
of bad fashion choices and mythical family locales

and then one day the family
just disintegrated
i was left with the father/husband
no longer couch adjacent
but shoved in the back
of a cheap atlanta storage unit

by the second summer
pictures from the 70's and 80's
were nothing but puddles
of yummy chemicals in my belly
to slowly digest

by the third summer i was in a landfill
where i could freely devour
the entire catalog of their lives

URBAN OASIS

in the complex
from my bedroom window
the gloomy metropolis was visible
through the patented atlanta haze
cars sardined into the parking lot
booming bass from trunks
where the street-pharmacist
hoop heroes and hard-core
anger junkies looking to scrap
all roamed those speed bumps
until dawn

there was no escape
for us latchkey nomads
stuck out here
on a naked blacktop wasteland
held up in our apartments
we took thirty-second vacations
in disney world commercials
eye-strolled up white sandy beaches
shaded under emerald-fingered palms
concepts as obscure as nature itself
to us tennis-shoe afterschool
cartoon warriors

but we did find some respite
just down the hill
behind a woven wall of pine
beneath a waterfall

of silver-haired kudzu
that splashed
onto a blue-green pasture
a drainage ditch stretched
before us like a nile

we retreated here
behind the nectar draped air
under a canopy of hemlocks,
sycamores and cottonwoods
where water gurgled
over the trash mosaic creek bottom
we would ski down
the steep muddy banks
skip silt-sopped stones
use a line, a hook, and our hands
to reel in mutated catfish
survey cavernous sewage pipes
all while discussing the big things
like which cereal is best
or the actress we would marry
or which drug dealer
drove the dopest ride

down here, we were safe
in a pocket of nature
and disney
and the apartment complex
and everything else up the hill
all seemed obscure

BRILLIANT PIGMENTS

Do colors
have brains?
Does red have a head
on its shoulders?
Can pink think?
Does gray conceive
that it matters?
If I picked
an intellectual color
it'd be green
for chloroplast
of course,
efficient energy,
no green people left
except for ill whites.
Nah, the genius hue
is regal blue,
blue people
would be Atlanteans
with cities built back
in thirty thousand BC
laughing at our color
coordinated lives.

Here, in 1990
Atlanta
(or is the second nine
upside down?)
did my classmate,

who calls himself friend,
really just pay me
the compliment of being
the smartest colored
he ever met?
Did I really just croak back
an instinctual: thank you?
Instead of: too bad I can't
say the same.
No   down here,
I've learned to keep
my brown mouth
(which the world sees
as black)   shut.

NOMADIC
for Mom

they find idols in her image
curved and carved
all over the old world

we are the same
round souls and bounce
the four corners with her

besides, nothing to keep us
here but tending rot,
weathering blows, why not leave?

it's cold and away,
but migration
for the sake of sanity's peace
is as inevitable as climate shifts

one day we live
in a garden
of divorcees
next we live
next to a drug den

even if returned
we will never weather
his sweltering droughts too long

so we have to go back
to being content on the move
packing up quick
carrying life on our backs

easy, this is what we were
built for

FACE BLINDNESS

me and my brown skin
are a novel topic
when i first arrive
at a southern indiana school
everyone goes out of their way
that first day

for me, i'm overwhelmed
by the barrage of pale
no bussing here
i was living amongst 'them'
so i had to make adjustments

especially out in the real world
at the sizzlers,
the malls, and the fall fairs
because when i waved
at 'friends,' i guess my face
would melt into a brown splotch
to be scared of   avoided
or just seen through
next day they would act
like nothing happened

when i came home hurt,
mom pulled me aside
and said, 'it does no good
trying to be buddies

with people who
don't *have* to see you.
just flatten them people
into the background
and keep on walking'

and i did
transforming my world
into a giant obstacle course
teaming with two-
legged obstructions
that i would simply
whitewash away
exactly like my friends
who i assumed
were taught these ways
by their parents, too

ACUTE AQUAPHOBIA

she was from the Camden New Jerz
elbow-dropped the vowels in her words
        so nice

a spire in pink crushed velour track tights
came to Indiana itching for bare knuckle fights
        I passed

she puffed up, threatening to beat my ass
thought I was uppity I thought she was crass
        and cruel

she told me don't show up at the pool
in our flat I watched it all summer through
        a window

mom wanted to know
why we moved all the way out here fo'
if I wasn't going to use the complex's amenities?

I told her why, then mom said to me
that girl gotta be sweet on you
and she masquerading it with bullying

eww, gross, now I had
two reasons not to go swim

MIA MCKENZIE

i had filed that god stuff away
into the saint nick/tooth-fairy bin
until mia mckenzie
came to magazine street church
and made me love alliteration
and god again

god had brought her as dark as a milky way
with a long midnight-black mane
vaseline-smeared baby-hair bangs
and always a proper sabbath bonnet

life became sabbath to sabbath
got baptized a week after her
joined bible bowl, learned useless trivia
from micah to elisha
so she'd think i was smart

but she never came to those
a.y.s. youth-centric afternoon events
i joined the pathfinders
because i liked the outdoors
but also heard she went on campouts
and imagined wooing her
with my tent-building skills

transferred to that understaffed
and underfunded church school
to get fluent in ellen g. white

going to church five nights a week
just to stare at her
and imagine us married
whatever that meant
ruling over her and home?
according to our bible studies

i even was her brother's best friend
i never heard her voice speak once
never looked her directly in the eye
never got invited to their house for dinner

and then abruptly, she was not there
and a letter was read in church saying
they had moved to d.c.
i felt serrated stabs of regret
wondered if that's how job felt

prayed to god
to send me another girl modeled
after mia mckenzie
made by the lord for me
but god never did
just had me sit through
four-hour services
stunted my educational growth
at that shitty school
so i tossed god back
in that fiction bin again

DADDY WOULD BE LIKE

used to wait months
for a haircut
daddy played chicken
with that shapeless blob
atop my head gaining mass
i'd plead with daddy
that i needed a fade
daddy would be like
 when i was your age
 i had a' afro
 two times bigger
 mines grew for years
 not no months
 and it was beautiful
really dad? it was the 70's
afros were in style
so i scrimped and saved
my lunch money
until i bought
a taming pick

used to have three days
worth of school 'fits
and when they
started disintegrating
daddy handed me down
his outdated grown man
business attire

sending me to school
swimming in the deep end
of polyester shirts
and belled slacks
i'd get kicked out of class
on purpose to avoid the ridicule
i'd beg for new kid-sized gear
daddy would be like
    them clothes are sharp, boy
    besides who you trying
    to impress anyway?
i don't know, dad
i'm a preteen male
going through puberty
so maybe girls?

after my knock-off eastlands
fell apart on my feet
daddy spray painted
these canvas white
clearance-rack boots
shiny shit brown
and made me wear
them to school
their glossy coating
bubbled and cracked
leaving a brown flake
trail through school to me
i'd come home crying
daddy would be like

you just going to
outgrow them things
in six months anyways
besides if they were
your true friends—
no shit dad,
so i became
a juvenile cobbler
duct-taping the integrity
back into those exploded
boat shoes that i secretly
wore the rest of the year

used to see daddy
in front of a mirror
before work
closet rupturing with clothes
his hair freshly cut
his shoes gleaming
as he smiled staring
into the mirror
chanting this mantra
    i'm six-foot two
    bronzed skin
    wavy black hair
    built like a greek god
    good god
and i would respond
dad, what's up with this?
i got no kicks, no 'fits, no fade

daddy would be like
        boy if you
        want something
        then you work you
        fifty hours a week
        and you get you a nine to five
        then you can get you
        whatever the hell you want
my reply
dad, i'm only thirteen
he would just smile
and take me to mickey-dees
for a four-piece mcnugget

i tried to tie it all together
for somebody i was telling
about daddy the other day
explaining yeah, it was
rough but
i think he was trying
to make me better,
less shallow you know?
and that person was like
        nope, it just sounds
        like you got a cheap ass daddy

TOO OLD FOR RECESS

at a private
church school
too broke to conduct class
around two hours
into no adult supervision
we turned to self-rule
lord of the flies style

some of us naïve, bookish
8-bit gamers
pictured ourselves noble
we pixelated the world
and became bare lipped
luigis and marios searching
for princess peaches to rescue
from eighth-grade bowsers
in hopes we'd receive
a lip glossed achievement flag
on the cheek

we never asked the girls
what they thought,
we just grabbed the scruff
of their school uniforms
and pulled them from beneath
the throbbing thrust
of drenched preteen boys
and while some thanked

us most yelled
we weren't their bosses either

and the big boys
atop the food chain
stayed on autopilot
grinding until they found
anything or anyone more tactile
than air to octopus around
and smother
even would be heroes
sometimes got snagged

YAGURL

comes up to me and this brotha
and tells him he looks like martin
  (he looks nothing like martin)
i start laughing
she getsallmad
her look sayin'
  they neva 'preciate nothing we give 'em
my brotha breaksitdown for yagurl
  'nobody ever told me that.
  they usually say i look like malcolm
  cause of the glasses'
she looks pissed off
  'well, i ain't never seen him!'
he looks at the ground and chuckles
hysterically i laugh
her body language is saying
  you try to be nice to these people
  'oh, now i remember. you do
  look like that malcolm x guy. i always
  get him mixed up with that king guy'
yagurl smiles and turns
and like magic
poof!
she acts like we disappear

I CHILL (da remix)

rollin' in somebody's ride, laid back
sippin' on a peach nehi
munchin' outa a grippo sac
quick to make that broadway scene
pumpin' da limits of my speaker machine
posse packed-in bumpin' to da beat
slacks hang black kicks on my feet
peepin' out da girls
they lookin' real ill
but i ain't stoppin' i gotta chill

i chill even though they try to stop that
po-pos skid up quick to hit with that billy club bat
life's like that people always buggin'
all they worry about are the problems they luggin'
they see a crew hangin' all cool-n-tight
they blow a fuse quick to ignite a fight
but that's the hand life's gonna deal
and while othas cop out
i choose to chill

ANOTHA KICK THEME

i went to school
pj 100s sneakers
strapped to my feet
they brand new
bought from one of those marts

but when the brothas
scope out my kicks
they laugh
because on they feet
they sporting $100 sneaks
in arrays of colors and styles
       pumped up
       aired out
       lit up
       gelled together
       and disc'd around

of course they got matching socks
they laugh at my tube socks
point at my non-namebranders
wipe the dust off their pseudo-suede kicks
that the striped-shirt salesman
claimed was real
to sucker in another $100 deal

even sista talk about me
not giving me the time of day

evidently i don't have any money
so i and my pj 100s are kicked to the curb

i don't get it
my sneaks are pleather
their sneaks are pleather
they just paid
the extra hundred for the
      swoosh and the air
      star and the gel
      claw and the disc
      gear and the lights
      name and the pump

and they just mad
'cause my kicks got way more attention
than theirs

DEAL WIT' IT

saw *roots*
got mad as hell
punk called me nigger
i kicked his ass
teach' said
   your kind has done nothing for america
i cussed her out
that's how i dealt wit' it

hanging with the brothas
i learned a new way to deal wit' it
seeing *roots* again
i learn from it
grow from it
punk calls nigger at me
i don't answer
that's not my name
teachers start spitting their crap
i don't hear it

i gather the younger brothas
and tell them
   without blacks, america wouldn't exist
and they learn a new way to
   deal wit' it

OLD SCHOOL

dj standin' in they dj stance
scratchin' up the wax
'cause they fresh to entrance
mc bustin' rhymes on the mike
why? cause they def tonight

boomboxes bumpin' always jammin'
crowd were jumpin' it was slammin'
b-boys beeboxin' on the TARC
breakdancers back spinnin' at the park
all was a part of this urban groove
and the only way to join was to bust-a-move!

clothes that were worn were dope as hell!
puma's, fila's, adidas gazelle's
bustin' out with the parachute slacks
kool herc fishnet shirts on their backs
people swingin' their curly hair
drip juice splashin' everywhere

the year I recall was '83
whodini, run dmc
fat boys, slick rick, kool moe dee
got a little play on mtv
for dropping that knowledge
hey-hey-hey-yo!
n-datz how dey made dey doe
rappin' about the wild wild west
roxanne roxanne was the best

also rap started movie makin'
beat street, krush groove, even *breakin'*
but then rap began repeatin'
the truth in the songs began depletin'
who knows why it lost its desire
next thing you know hip-hop is on fire
hip-hop   hip-hop   hip-hop is on fire

we couldn't afford no water
so we had to let it burn . . .

MR. NAP'S FIGHT

brothas and sistas never gave you dap
you rose from the scalp
of the black gene pool
but since you ain't stringy you ain't too cool
so the first people yank you with afro picks
cook ya clean-straight with hot comb tricks
so you could be manageable
                    at least for a day
after work and sweat
                    you come back anyway

so to combat on you some more
folks chemically bombarded
you with conks galore
get a perm every four to six weeks
but you still bulge and you peek
through that mop of devilish straight hairs
look like we got you in noose snares

you're drowned in jheri-curl juice spray
electric clippers grind you into a stubbled grave
stocking caps suppress you into bumpy waves
straight asian bobs slipped over african knobs
disguising you so we can stay in school
                    and keep our jobs

horsetails bring up a debate
stapled, braided, or glued-in at a snail's rate
you're bleached farrah fawcett gold
                 or dyed at your roots
but you continue on with the spending
                 of much much loot

all done to keep you down
but mr. naps...   you still hang around?
making appearances in
'fros, naturals, and dreads
keeping a strong presence
                 on the face of *our* heads

MY NATURE

thanks asphalt
you spawned me
cradled me
taught me
disciplined me
you were my grass
telephone poles my trees
sewage drains my brooks
my tenement unit a spacious chalet
that mountainous billboards and
church steeples overlooked
you were my inspiration
for spitting stories
my affrilachia
my feets will glide over you
running into peeps
only you could produce
where money's good
but most survive without too much
asphalt   where i have been
and always will be
in my mind at least
'cause in this whacked world
i got to have a spot i can go
and be myself
where i can go
and just   chill

ENGLISH LIT

english lit
ain't never meant shit
     to me
          a griot
from urban decay
i care less
about the way
the middle english
or even
their contemporaries display
their masturbation a.k.a.
mastery of a native tongue
sprung from spliced together
stolen components
of failed
conquest-thirsty cultures

meanwhile
i carry a' eighty-dollar
         leather bound
     fifty-pound edition
that i don't even read
sitting in classrooms
full of white girls
who aspire to be teachers
or pontificating writers
like the self-absorbed ones
up front

jackin' their egos
for hours straight
about imagined intricate
insignificant details
of forced literary regurgitation
and their slightly different
postmodern imitations

they talk about my limitation
on papers
and in my daily speech
yet i still continue
to reach to the streets
representin'
even though
they be hintin'
with C–'s and D+'s
that my attempts at writing
should cease and desist

but my claim to fame
is not only as a writer
but also an arsonist
because every time
that my pen and paper hit
i receive great joy at watchin'
the queen's english
being lit

I STILL RIDE THE TARC

i still ride the tarc buses
   with their pissy smelling seats
   gum stuck to feet

odor of butt and malt liquor
overhead fluorescent light flickers

     back bench full of shopping bags
     seats tattooed with graffiti tags

redundant ringing of stop bells
old vets spittin' tall tales

     lames in fly-away collars
     dudes peeping girls itching to holla

grease spots on the window that seeped from hair
from bums stretched out asleep who just don't care

     little bad-ass kids' screams
     old lady evil-eye beams

headphones blastin' until ears are sore
old transfers and pay stubs littering the floor

     disproportionate abundance of the black race
     bus drivers clutching cans of mace

89

when shipping us goods from the hoods to malls
this concrete ship rarely stalls

rushin' us to serve on the trip out
our bodies be in-route

economically packed
from the front to the back

and them raising prices all the time
to be middle-passage confined

in the belly of the steel beast
and when us suburban laborers are released

by drivers late they demonstrate an attitude
that's when i get rude

because on the way back to our shanty township
the buses break down and be ill-equipped

worn seat vinyl and bald tires
and drivers who in two days will retire

so i get home at midnight
my work-journey hours equaling ten

and the next day... guess what?
i gotta do it all again

just the blahzay-blahzay on the tarc every day
why? it's my only way

WELCOME WAGON

netting 15k a year barely affords me
a $375 a month one bedroom
free basic cable, gruel walls and floors

amenities include: gunplay in the parking lot
trunk bass knocking if it's dark or not
and narcotic available at the laundromat

she heads the apartment greeting committee
she lives below me in unit 1-b
a red-wigged gargoyle with hummingbird arms
that only pause when she drags off her infinite Newport
conversing and sometime scuffling
with beings not even there
as she guards our building's front stoop

she will never bring up
a 'hello neighbor' casserole
or nice bottle of vino
just the aroma of ammonia
and melting plastics
just offers of 'halfsies' on nuggets
at two a.m. runs to Wendy's

sometimes she runs suicide drills
on her coffee table
sometimes she screams
so long and so loud

that a portal opens
and she enters it disappearing for weeks
but she always returns with a new color wig
a new adventure to go on

and that's the welcome part

MY MALL

through a glass
and brass portal
i take flight
on superiority trips
in my own mind
i define myself
by new gear
gadgets
and status wealth
mass produced
to seduce
loose in capitalism
at its peak
surrounded by bags
bugged
with brand-name goods
that i bartered
my soul for

in the midst of
xerox people
collated
laminated
fresh off the press
imitating a one-dimensional
high profiled
media styled
cookie cutter existence
where fads and culture

are interchangeable concepts
created to move products

here   i am absorbed
sucked of
color
individuality
and far from home
i try to be equal
as i'm barely considered
human   here
but my green is enough
for a censored copy
of the american dream
that i stroll through
with tracking devices
sewn into the swooshes
of my nikes

i act like this place is mine
pressing my too-big sneakers
into the tiny drone footprints
marching up and down
the corridors
of this 72-degree
window-shopping tropics
a polyester slice of nature
between boxed-up nylon wishes
surrounded by a blacktop tundra

and i stop
because this place
ain't mine
because if it was
i wouldn't be getting here by bus
and when i step through
any door of any store
i wouldn't get every eyeball on me
initiating a security red alert

MY PEOPLES BELIEVE IN WORK

i remember
big sis
coming in
smelling of onions and taco meat
working 'til one a.m.
on a school night
talking about she *a slave for da man*
at the time i wondered who the man was
mom and dad hollering
because she spent all her
paychecks on clothes and stuff

later i remember
other big sis
coming home late
bragging about straight a's
after three hours of chorus
and four hours of work
hands all rough and dry
mom and dad praising her
she saved her 'revenue'
in a bank for college
so she could sing her way
out of a nine to five

a few years later at sixteen
tired of pulling nothing but
lint from my pockets
i started putting in hours after school

at a variety of fast food shacks
ideal of being a writer
sprouting in my head
clocking in at four p.m.
and not leaving 'til close
                i didn't like it
giving my hours away
for money
i ended up giving back
to the same folks anyway
mom and dad shaking their
heads because my dollars
were in jars under the bed
and i was always screaming
i ain't going to be doing this
for the rest of my life!
working forty hours a week
for forty years
just so i can die
with a fat pocket
a nice car
and a house in the hills
that ain't me
i need to stand for something

nowadays big sis
say a little something about
being a slave
after a forty-hour work week
other big sis
mentions those a's

sometimes
after cleaning houses eight hours a day

and i wonder
do they still stand for something?
and will i?

THE 19 AT MIDNIGHT

i used to anticipate it, back when it was me and
ole dude drenched in darkness and aroma of fast
food, our soaked pants legs spanking ankles, our
pastel poly-blended polo's plastered with grease,
condiments, and corporate insignias, as our indigo
fingers, inked from clocking out, juggled cobalt
quarters waiting for that 19 to chug up to our stop.

all the while, like he was training, ole dude would
bestow ghetto lessons, like slit the baloney before
you fry it or channel miss daisy's hoke when you
see them blue lights.

through swinging bus doors and up the stairwell
of the 19 at midnight, our rolling reprieve was
always standing room only, an after-work hangout
for a people without one. for a 75-cent cover we
saw more life on there than in any nightclub we
couldn't get into.

we'd head to the back, fluorescent lights staring
down from the ceiling illuminating people dressed
like me, smelling like me, from old cats talking
80's smack to worn women filling two-thirds of the
vinyl benches deflecting the constant advances of
most men under fifty.

then after leaving st. matthews, maybe after a hit
off a roach or a rock or a sip of schlitz, ole dude
would get tilted, bantering and bartering, smuggled
surplus six pieces in original or crispy, paired with
biscuits in swollen fogged-up ziplocks for either
half of a sbarro's pepperoni or a stack of big macs
or a fiver (he called it 'picking up dinner for my
bullback snow bunny').

we'd all feast and would be halfway content with
that hour-long nightly event detached from time
at least for a few miles, and i could see how this
made   here   more tolerable.

then one day i came to work after class and boss
tre with the receding hairline and gums said he
fired ole dude 'for being dumb enough to get locked
up for beating down a fat white chick.' again, a
proxy daddy winds up being counterfeit. another
million half-assed lessons to unlearn.

after that i didn't anticipate a torturous work
commute home every day anymore. i just got on
that 19 & ali and stood dead asleep with my eyes
wide open all the way home, until i could graduate
out of   there.

RITES OF TRAFFIC

has happened a million times before
seedy part of town
two a.m. strip clubs just closed
two black men   no headlights
get their inevitable
inaugural violation stop

four black-and-whites converge
a dozen public servants deploy
hands on gun butts
trigger fingers trembling
flashlights tight beamed
searching every inch
the two men are eyes wide
stone-bodied in bucket seats

all of a sudden   an officer yells
    is that a titty?   ha!
    these boys in here
    looking at nudie magazines!

then all the fellas have a good laugh
    about some *naked sluts*
and the men get off with just a warning but a
    we've got our eyes on you boys
as the drift of cops saunter away

HOLLYWOOD

elevated
bigger than life
hot pink letters
etched into night
on that side of town
no schools or churches
were found
but blue movie stores
and neon signs
speckled the blackness
it was la-la land
just ten minutes away

we give casting calls
on the edge of
brass-barred stages
with teeth-clenched dollars
slipped between soft,
supple orbs
looking for leading ladies
to co-star with us
they audition into
the silver panoramic
frames that line the
walls and ceilings
we verbally contract a deal
financed by us
shooting on-location in our laps
in a secluded shag-carpeted

booth on a velvet red couch
the actress with the seductive
stage name
gives an impromptu
choreographed routine
just like a musical
only it costs twenty dollars
to make
and is only two songs long

at the wrap
she places our last twenty
in her garter with the rest
and proceeds to edit us
onto the plush
alcohol drenched
cutting room floor

TEMP TO HIRE

banners hang from strip mall rafters
between sprint stores and starbucks
staffing agencies' promise of
ten-dollars-an-hour positions
enticing recent grads
transitioning to disenfranchised
trying to get a foot in
trying to cash in those priceless degrees
for pennies on the dollar
at these one-stop job shops

applicants become
digital john henries of data entry
sledgehammer fingers clobbering keys
head-to-head racing
steam-powered phantom robot typist
to forty words per minute

pee drug-free in a plastic cup
and in two weeks
win the prize
report to work

POET VS. CORPORATE ME

he waits   to smelt his pain
back there   with imagination
to ambush   for pennies
with silk slip knots   he smiths words
to starched-collar shackles   and hopes for a full stomach
he wants his body back
to homestead   to submit and get rejected by
cubicle farms and   asphyxiating journals, to entertain
bouncing ergonomic chairs   into debt black holes for degrees
off of glass ceilings   of separation to become a literary elite?
punching clocks   for no real dollars just a jaded dream
instead of air   selling himself by the earfuls
admiration for his pluck
after all these years
is the only reason i keep him around

SAVING POEMS

how many poems
have scintillated
like day-stars
on the yellow horizon
a quick flicker
at stifling
afternoon
staff meetings

how many poems
have sat on my nose tip
gnome big
staring me down
through one more
tv show binge
only to be smashed
into my pores
when i pass out
and roll over on them

how many poems
have latched within
my nether hairs, gnawing
picked up in the woods
camped out somewhere
then washed
down the drain
at my next hot shower
how many poems

have leapt on my eyelids
heavy with hip curves
dancing
in smoke-shadows
dissipating
from my mouth

those poems go free
and explore
how lucky

but most
if caught
become birdcage liner
forgotten
under the downpour
of more and more

RECYCLING NEIGHBORHOODS

'new park duvalle'
always just duvalle
since i was born
now rebranded
regentrified
a sugared outer shell
of pastel vinyl cloned homes
on postage-stamp lots
crowding and dashing into
interstate-obstructed horizons,
barred in by the shadows
of coal ash smokestacks
here backyard gardens
grow out of the rubble
of plowed-over projects

southwick and cotter homes projects
a fifty-year experiment
i grew up adjacent to
named for the white developer
who always owned this land
and the black mayor
of the town sacrificed
for this monstrosity
of terra cotta buildings
knotted up and down
the single potholed street
dead-ending
at a police station

where cops were soldiers
doing tours of duty
in *that little africa shithole*

'little africa'
sometimes called 'black parklands'
other times 'needmore'
forgotten hamlet of freed slaves
self-governed
self-educated
with planked streets
brown brick businesses
wooden cottages crammed
and cobbled to the river
community growing
like an orange trumpet vine
from the bogged black earth
of this once bypassed marsh

ignored avoided swamp,
nameless estuary
too many mosquitos
too much stink
to do anything here
back before emancipation
before beargrass creek
became our sewer
and it still flowed
through the middle
of what is now downtown

feeding enough fertile sediment
to build the first louisville upon
before corn island, too,
got all used up by this city
leaving only a spangle of stones
visible when the ohio river
is shrunken by drought

ALL RELATIVE

people ask what it was like
being a cousin of the greatest
I shoot back: I know what you know
spoken word histories
recited over haircuts by barber bards
infectious sound bites and micro poems
elaborately staged fights
and bucking the whole establishment

I did actually meet him once though
back when summer
would hang all my sisters and me
out the car door windows like dog tongues
we rolled through downtown
when daddy stomped the brakes
and next thing we know
daddy's hollering *Cassius!*
and we're cutting a line of white people
to meet this man
who looks the same model as daddy
just different trim
he has a self-portrait sketched on his shirt
and the words THE GREATEST
stretched tight across his chest
he poses for a picture with just me
his fist the same size as my head
raised to my chin
in a ruddy polaroid
my only proof we met

the other time was barely a rendezvous
I was in high school and at war with the world
and myself
when he returned to central high, his alma mater
an afro messiah barely able to murmur
but happily struggling to still raise his shrunken fist
to a crowd of strangers' chins just like he had done
with me in that now-lost polaroid
I left without saying a word, angry,
blaming everything but jealousy
because I thought our connection was special

that last time
I was in his physical presence
it had been so long
I had almost forgotten
he was my second cousin
he was hidden in this box draped black
and gold stitched with arabic calligraphy
I hardly felt anything
as relatives posed with his casket
for social media

so I left the service and went deep
into the west end where we all come from
and biking through the people-lined streets
was a swarm of pedal-propelled butterflies
all of us he touched
all of us who got goosebumps
when he dazzled a mic

all of us with polaroids of some sort
posed with him raising a fist to our chins
and it was then I knew I wasn't his family
because of my blood or my last name
I was his family because he made his
block, his city, this world, his family

MAKING OF A CASUAL ASTRONOMER

From my yard, I could only count a few dozen
tiny twinkled suns shining through the patchy
purple above. Incandescent smog stunted my
night vision for so many years, I didn't see my
first Milky Way until the radiantly rain-danced
renditions of the heavens were splayed across
planetarium ceilings foretelling that once-in-a-
lifetime snowball that would hang on the horizon
for weeks next year. In anticipation I asked Santa
for a telescope, dreaming of anti-gravity summer
camps in Huntsville and walking on the moons
of Saturn one day. I aimed to follow the footsteps
of Ronald McNair, until that crisp January
morning when they broadcast into my third-grade
classroom that shuttle bursting into an orange
fireball then plumes of white through the ice blue
sky. It challenged my celestial ambitions. After
that, I was content to pinhole project total solar
eclipses onto index cards and hike parsecs into the
wild at dusk, to recline back into indigo meadows
or be embraced by black bluffs as my silvering
eyes filled up with stars.

BERNHEIM FOREST, EARLY SPRING

the pink and white and the lilac and the dogwood
and the pear and the redbud are lace fastened to
the blue and frolic under the spiny green horizon.
on rare weekends we took day trips out of the
humming city with daddy and the orange volvo
wagon jammed with family and ice-packed coolers
filled with black cherry big-k sodas, funyuns,
and tuna salad. out there pondside at spongy
picnic tables when the chewing stopped, we could
hear the sun barreling through space, hear the
tree buds opening above, hear the red-bellied
woodpeckers' warble rolling from their speckled
throatlash, or just hear nothing at all.

BORN TREKKER

when i'm cradled in green
trail runners drumming dirt on universal beat
my hiking poles pistoning
when people see me out there
say, the canyons of kauai, or a conifer
forest in arizona, or an elk prairie in the smokies

i get the same look, like i just pissed the pool
like, what the hell are you doing here?
then they want to school me
on proper outdoor etiquette

like, these places, these national parks, these back
country trails, these paradises aren't for
people like me, who are the color of wood and earth

which is funny, because if you go back
you'll see these parks and wildernesses
were second surveyed by buffalo-skinned people like
me   and for that matter
going back even further
                         so was the entire world

ALLERGEN

this trip
i'm plagued with
sneezing and congestion
surprising up here
in appalachia's
seemingly pristine air
must be my hay fever flaring up
over those seldom spoken about
invasive steel plants
that jut up
in boxy barbed thickets
along barren river banks and
carved into the foot of naked mountains
like titan dandelions
spewing white feather-like pappus hairs
from shiny stems into the sky
to become clouds
carrying a secret pollen
seeding countless
cancer and asthma cluster blossoms
itching my eyes
until they water
every time
i see one of those weeds

APPALACHIAN SMITTEN

though she is more mature
than her terrestrial sisters
        rocky, andes, or himalaya
though osteoporosis has set in
on her nooks and valleys
she still survived
mastectomies daily for decades
she is so grand
not all her tears are slurry
some of her kisses
are still spring pure
her rain-worn curves
still the smoothest
i've ever explored
still framing some of my
most sensual moments
geologically speaking
she is lena horne
regal   eternal   beauty

THE LISTENING

never heard stone fences before
didn't know they had a voice
but here they were
on a kentucky roadside
screaming at me
as i took a rural bypass
jaggedly snaking up the road
parallel to my car
sharp, gapped, gleaming
limestone teeth dipping and rising
they lay buoyed
in an ocean of bluegrass
inviting me to investigate
to step off the asphalt shore
into the rip current
of the vast green sea
as i got closer to those chiseled
dry assembled stone hedges
the loudening
of woven palm prints
invisibly inked
just below the stone surfaces
filled me with a familiar sound
heard faintly when gazing
upon pictures of pyramids
or olmec heads
or stonehenge
it's the diaspora's continuum
transcending space and time

linking me
to primordial rock masons
they mortared themselves
into these craggy borders
to hold this place together
i imagine a world
where i could stop here
without fear of a noose
or bullet
where i could wade out
among the thoroughbreds
as i rub the bouldered faces
listening to the petrified walls
i feel their pebbly pores,
close my eyes, light drizzling
from the sky between clouds
heating my face
as the chatter is swallowed
by the cars
passing like waves

WHAT IS PASSED ON
for Bernard Sr.

by the time I came
the stockyards had severed a number
of granddaddy's fingertips
and a bullet from an ex-employee
of the butcher shop he owned
had blasted a fragment out of his nose

my little sister and I
sat on his lap
and played in the dimpled scar
right below his cloudy slate eyes
I hardly recall him talking much
just his omnipresent laugh

he valued hard work over conversation
taught me how to maul a log
dig a fence post
strip and paint a house
he was elbow grease personified
building a garage from scratch
near the end of his life

that last time at thanksgiving
for the first time ever
he told me about his daddy Rube
an entrepreneur with dark skin
who sold huge blocks of ice

dragging them in a wagon
with his kids
behind an ornery mule
all over louisville

and when the beast got stubborn
Rube would take his fist
and clobber down
on the top of that mule's head
knocking it on its butt
nothing stopped Rube
he always sold every cube
and that's where Ali got that strength
and that drive from
and you have it, too, Bernie
grandaddy said ending the parable
before he dozed off in his recliner

satisfied but wanting more
I knew he'd be around to provide
so I went back
to playing with my cousins
a week later I was in front of a coffin
granddaddy's face muted behind a veil
my stomach in my throat
my thoughts lingered on that final meal
that last and only story

now I channel him
whenever effort is called for

every time I spade a swale by hand
every time I haul a load on my back
every time I split a log into splinters
every time I roll up my sleeves
to form a story
I resurrect him

Acknowledgments

For Mom and Dad, the black sheep of your families, who paired up and taught Vonne, Angie, Vette and me it was good to be different. You are all my foundation · For Lauren, you never let me give up this infinite pursuit of storytelling · For my extended family and friends, always there when it counted · For Louisville, your segregated grids forged me · For Kentucky, your unrealized potential propels me · For Ms. Bundrant, in third grade you encouraged me to write not as an assignment, but out of love of stories · For Dee Hawkins, you saw a poet through all my angst at Central High · For Frank X Walker, you gave me the blueprint for writing about my reality, about family · For Crystal Wilkinson, Kelly Norman Ellis, and the rest of the Affrilachian Poets, you shape and inspire me · For Nikky Finney, you taught me to relentlessly hunt for truth with our art form · For Gurney Norman, your lessons on narrative imbue this collection, meshing imagination with memory · For Julia Johnson and the UK MFA program, for accepting me · For the Swanbergs, for enabling my journey through the Nikky Finney Graduate Fellowship · For upfromsumdirt, the cover is dope as hell · For Nyoka Hawkins, your support, patience and vision on this long but beautiful journey to a collection has been invaluable · For these poems, I don't own you. We started meeting when I was a teen and have been gathering over the decades like family. I was lucky enough to raise you with the guidance of the people above. My hope now: that you go out into the world and speak to someone, impassion someone, tickle someone, and just be.

About the Author

BERNARD CLAY was born in the shadow of the now demolished Southwick housing projects in the West End of Louisville, Kentucky. He spent most of his childhood and high-school years in Louisville, living for brief periods in Georgia and Indiana. He received an MFA in Creative Writing from the University of Kentucky in 2017 and is a member of the Affrilachian Poets collective. He currently lives on a farm in eastern Kentucky with his wife Lauren. *English Lit* is his first book.

English Lit was designed by Nyoka Hawkins. Cover art by upfromsumdirt/Ronald Davis. The text was set in New Aster, a typeface designed in 1958 by Francesco Simoncini. The cover typeface is Ysans, designed in 2017 by Jean François Porchez. Grateful acknowledgment to Stephanie Adams and Sharon Hatfield for editorial assistance.